# pocket posh®
· · · · · · · · · ·
# take care

Inspired Activities
for **Mindfulness**

# pocket posh
· · · · · · · · ·
# take care

## Inspired Activities
## for **Mindfulness**

**Andrews McMeel**
PUBLISHING®

We all need some time to focus on ourselves. It's easy to become overwhelmed—by work, by home responsibilities, by the news of the day. It's important to step away, relax, and recenter. *Take Care: Inspired Activities for Mindfulness* invites you to practice small moments of self-care through mindful activities, inspirational words, and thought-provoking journal prompts. Take some time for yourself.

. . . take care.

"Let's be brave enough
to dream big, huge,
embarrassingly
impossible dreams."

*—Melody Ross*

```
D D E A G E R G F U P L E A S U R E G J
A F M S D P O P R I D E Z D O J A S C O
R N T E L E F U N E D Z E D R I B A D Y
O O D N W A N C S M S T X E O D J T I J
U K H S T M U H Z C N L T R E T A I S U
S L X I E A G O V A A T Y T L N S S G B
E I Z T P Z A N H V I R A Y J Q D F U I
D V M I E E D C Q B Y R E R P E N I S L
R E N V N D N R U X E D L D M X K E T A
S L F E T E R G Y B Y T A A C A L D V N
I Y D W H X D X I A F U H M X H W D W T
P F H P U W E L U H Y S T E R I C A L E
E H C K S S U A M L A R P P G L A Z Y I
L S M A I P X G Y A P U Z Z L E D R B R
E V W J A Q T I O H L R A A X L I N A E
V G K Q S M R T C N A N C A N G E R Y J
A O G N T G G A L Z X H S E J Z H R G H
R H D M I M A T L I E C S T A T I C S R
E Q X P C W W E R U B R E L I E F G Y B
B S C M S I U D W T M J P V T Y V W M T
```

## emotions

| | | |
|---|---|---|
| AGITATED | ENCHANTED | PRIDE |
| AMAZED | ENTHUSIASTIC | PUZZLED |
| ANGER | HYSTERICAL | RELIEF |
| AROUSED | JOY | SATISFIED |
| ASHAMED | JUBILANT | SCARED |
| BITTER | LAZY | SENSITIVE |
| DISGUST | LIBERATED | SEXY |
| EAGER | LIVELY | |
| ECSTATIC | PLEASURE | |

# mindful every day

We often associate mindfulness with things such as yoga and meditation, but you don't have to take a class or go to a special studio to incorporate mindfulness into your day. Mindfulness is all about being present in your own life—focusing on what's happening in your present moment, not anxieties about the future or ruminating on the past. It's being fully aware of your actions and thoughts as they happen: when you eat, focus on the sensations and tastes of your food; when you're outside, pay attention to the sounds and smells of your environment; when you're talking to a friend, be an active listener. Practicing making these small shifts in your mindset can lead to big changes in overall happiness.

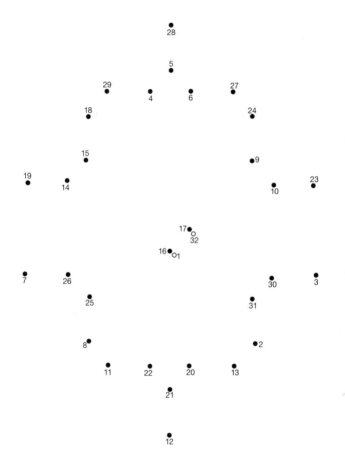

# mindful gratitude exercise

Practicing gratitude has been proven to improve emotional and physical health. When we take the time to stop and appreciate the good in our lives, we reframe our perspective. Expressing gratitude, even for the smallest things, can lead to big change.

What is something in your physical environment that you are grateful for (for example, your favorite piece of art, a treasured family heirloom, or even a comfy chair)?

. . . . . . . . . . . . . . . . . . . . . . . . . . . . . . . . . . . . . . . . . . . . . . . .

. . . . . . . . . . . . . . . . . . . . . . . . . . . . . . . . . . . . . . . . . . . . . . . .

. . . . . . . . . . . . . . . . . . . . . . . . . . . . . . . . . . . . . . . . . . . . . . . .

. . . . . . . . . . . . . . . . . . . . . . . . . . . . . . . . . . . . . . . . . . . . . . . .

. . . . . . . . . . . . . . . . . . . . . . . . . . . . . . . . . . . . . . . . . . . . . . . .

. . . . . . . . . . . . . . . . . . . . . . . . . . . . . . . . . . . . . . . . . . . . . . . .

"Always keep your eyes open.
Keep watching. Because whatever
you see can inspire you."

—*Grace Coddington*

## COOKING By Will Nediger

### ACROSS

1. Salma of "Frida"
6. Most common, statistically
11. All together
12. "Schitt's Creek" star Catherine
13. What a good meal provides, physically and spiritually
15. Curly corn chips
16. Stir-fry vessel
17. "That proves it!"
18. Double agent
19. With 21-Across, spiritual sustenance, or a style of African-American cuisine
21. See 19-Across
22. Golf target
23. Attracted to all genders, for short
24. Come to a close
25. Excited Spanish cry
28. Food that often provides spiritual sustenance
31. PR concern
32. Gave, as a meal
33. Fancy abode
34. Released

### DOWN

1. Culture writer Karen
2. Starting from
3. "___ mileage may vary"
4. Julio Iglesias's son
5. Harvey of "Reservoir Dogs"
6. Scale of mineral hardness
7. Unit of resistance
8. Onetime Korean carmaker
9. ___ Palmer (iced tea/ lemonade drink)
10. Potato pancake
14. Chunk of lawn
18. Nickname
19. California wine valley
20. Dad, slangily
21. Way in the distance
22. Gender pronoun listing for many
23. No amateur
25. Taiwanese computer company
26. Wait
27. Pay to play poker
29. It might be massaged
30. Prayer addressee

"You're a diamond.
Never sell yourself
as coal."

—*Mina Rehman*

```
O G P C Q G S P R I N K L E R S T B W P
M B G O K G M S O X N E R T L M N O E I
F O H R A N K K S V R U N E J C H D V C
B S D N Y F U A H M E Z D G C V P K L N
F U L A A J A T U H O R S E S H O E S I
R O I C K H G E F V W K S O C C E R M C
I T V Q C N V B F Q R Q P A B W E P H S
S A Y A I B O O L T M G E H H A F A U I
B G E W S Q L A E R K D C P I T Q L L S
E B S Q B K L R B E R B R A D E P L A A
E V H E G Z E D O E O I O D E R A A H Q
R R T V U S Y M A C L C Q D A B D W O I
Q I A F W P B S R L L Y U L N A D N O O
K I K F J A A O D I E C E E D L L B P L
C R A X T F L R X M R L T B S L E O I X
W M C F L I L K K B S E M A E O B W U I
P Y A K R P N X X I K K Y L E O O L N Z
E M L M N P O G M N A X B L K N A I N F
B W S M O N Z O O G T C A X Y S R N S N
W B O C C E B A L L E G G D O N D G L G
```

## outdoor fun

| | | |
|---|---|---|
| BEACH | LAWN BOWLING | SOCCER |
| BICYCLE | PADDLEBALL | SPRINKLERS |
| BOCCE BALL | PADDLEBOARD | SWING |
| CROQUET | PARK | TAG |
| FRISBEE | PICNIC | TREE CLIMBING |
| HIDE-AND-SEEK | POOL | VOLLEYBALL |
| HORSESHOES | RAFTING | WALK |
| HULA-HOOP | ROLLER SKATE | WATER BALLOONS |
| KAYAK | SHUFFLEBOARD | |
| KITE | SKATEBOARD | |

```
R  G  E  N  O  A  Z  X  J  E  I  F
X  O  Z  M  A  Y  O  R  V  G  N  L
M  A  M  H  C  S  E  K  I  N  D  O
I  H  J  E  E  B  V  L  O  A  I  R
L  O  P  L  A  N  T  K  L  R  G  E
A  L  P  U  R  P  L  E  E  O  O  N
N  A  V  E  N  I  C  E  T  Z  W  C
N  P  A  L  E  R  M  O  V  G  B  E
```

## find and circle

| | |
|---|---|
| Seven large Italian cities | ⊘○○○○○○ |
| Five six-letter colors | ○○○○○ |
| City leader | ○ |
| Hawaiian "hello" and "good-bye" | ○ |
| Flower or shrub, for example | ○ |

"Life isn't about finding yourself. Life is about creating yourself."

—*George Bernard Shaw*

# body scan meditation

Simple meditation exercises can help bring about greater focus and clarity. Try to incorporate short meditation breaks into your day a few times a week and see what happens.

STEP 1: Close your eyes and concentrate on your breathing.

. . . . . . . . . . . . . . . . . . . . . . . . . . . . . . . . . . . . . . . . . .

STEP 2: Tune into the sensations in your body. You may think about feelings in your fingers or toes or the way your breath feels going in and out of your nose. You can systematically go through these sensations—for example, starting at the top of your head and working your way down to your toes—or explore freely, wherever your curiosity takes you.

. . . . . . . . . . . . . . . . . . . . . . . . . . . . . . . . . . . . . . . . . .

STEP 3: If you find your attention wandering, simply notice that fact *without judgment* and bring your focus back to your body.

. . . . . . . . . . . . . . . . . . . . . . . . . . . . . . . . . . . . . . . . . .

STEP 4: Continue until you have scanned your entire body. When you are finished, sit for a few moments more and when you are ready, open your eyes.

. . . . . . . . . . . . . . . . . . . . . . . . . . . . . . . . . . . . . . . . . .

1<sup>OO</sup>70

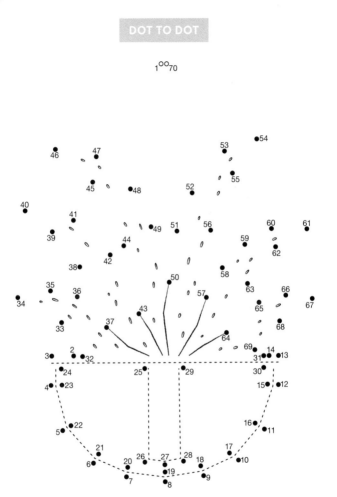

# walking meditation

You don't have to sit still to meditate. All mindfulness practices are simply about focusing your attention— and you can do that while going about your day, even while walking around. The goal is to develop relaxed attention to what is happening in your present moment.

Focus on your breath

· · · · · · · · · · · · · · · · · · · · · · · · · · · · · · · · · · · · · · · · · · ·

Concentrate on the sensation of your feet touching the ground

· · · · · · · · · · · · · · · · · · · · · · · · · · · · · · · · · · · · · · · · · · ·

Move your attention around your body, part by part, like a body scan meditation

· · · · · · · · · · · · · · · · · · · · · · · · · · · · · · · · · · · · · · · · · · ·

Notice any external sounds or smells around you

· · · · · · · · · · · · · · · · · · · · · · · · · · · · · · · · · · · · · · · · · · ·

If your mind wanders, gently bring your focus back to the present

· · · · · · · · · · · · · · · · · · · · · · · · · · · · · · · · · · · · · · · · · · ·

"Look at everything as though you were seeing it either for the first or last time. Then your time on earth will be filled with glory."

—*Betty Smith*

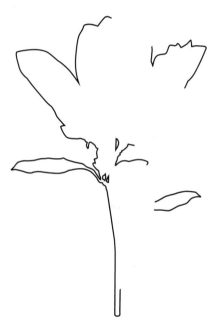

# FOREST BATHING By Will Nediger

## ACROSS

1. Observes Ramadan
6. Including on an email
11. Hayes or Newton
12. Knight covering
13. Sense for appreciating the feel of moss
14. Sense for appreciating the flavor of fresh berries
15. Amount that you make
17. It goes viral
18. Word before a maiden name
19. Super stoked
21. Home of the practice of forest bathing (where it's called "shinrin-yoku")
22. Widespread
25. Franchise with spinoffs set in Miami and New York
28. Landed
29. Sparkly headpieces
31. Sense for appreciating the look of light streaming through the canopy
33. Sense for appreciating the fragrance of pine needles
34. Gestation stations
35. Home made with hides
36. Evita's last name
37. Prone to fidgeting

## DOWN

1. Get along with the rest of a group
2. In unison
3. Pesto or mole
4. Alliterative Tuesday fare
5. Bagel topper
6. Purring pet
7. Pack tightly
8. "Are you ready?" response
9. "Who did this? response
10. Avarice
16. American in Paris, e.g.
20. Flockhart of "Ally McBeal"
21. Rock's ___ Tull
22. Fill the tank
23. Best of the best
24. African river with two countries named after it
25. Moved sneakily
26. Department that might have quotas
27. R&B's ___ Brothers
30. "You can say that again!"
32. Cookie holder

"Follow what you are
genuinely passionate about
and let that guide you to
your destination."

—*Diane Sawyer*

```
F R U I T E Y R E L A T I O N S H I P S
E V X E X E R C I S E R U R I T G P G M
E W M X S F O O Z H G T Z L X E T D I D
L H B H I M R C G W A O K Q D C L W G Y
E O O P B L E E J F L P O O K R A N P Q
A L N U E S A A S X I S O D L J I W J K
N E S T T E N B T H S F T U S N R Z K K
M G H M I S F N O B A D N R I L A H L A
E R O B A A I G J E R I M A E C E A I W
A A T S L L N D S G B E R I I T W E M P
T I T L T I L X E W H T A N L K C E P Z
S N E G G T K M B Q T X A K S K J H Y I
U S A G T X T W E H W G A I F V M U X P
S N O E N I R K G A R J R Q X A D F J P
G J M P B V M I R O L B Q L X D S X Q F
S O C A A B E X P W A S L P W J F T H B
A J H Z P W P M R M D R I N K W A T E R
J V E G E T A B L E S E D A I L Y Q D W
C J F A M I L Y I S H Z A S N A C K V X
R F R H Y D R A T E G V A R N Y C V Q T
```

being healthy

| | | |
|---|---|---|
| BRISK WALK | HABIT | SEAFOOD |
| DAILY | HOT TEA | SMALL MEALS |
| DRINK WATER | HYDRATE | SNACK |
| EAT BREAKFAST | JOGGING | STRETCH |
| EXERCISE | LEAN MEATS | VEGETABLES |
| FAMILY | MILK | WEIGHT TRAINING |
| FRESH AIR | ORGANIC | WHOLE GRAINS |
| FRUIT | OUTSIDE | |
| GOOD SLEEP | RELATIONSHIPS | |

# mindful connection

We all have people in our lives whose love and support make our lives better. Take a moment to think about them. Write down their names and what they mean to you. Try to reach out to these people in some way and express your feelings. Connection and community are priceless.

. . . . . . . . . . . . . . . . . . . . . . . . . . . . . . . . . . . . . . . . . . . . .

. . . . . . . . . . . . . . . . . . . . . . . . . . . . . . . . . . . . . . . . . . . . .

. . . . . . . . . . . . . . . . . . . . . . . . . . . . . . . . . . . . . . . . . . . . .

. . . . . . . . . . . . . . . . . . . . . . . . . . . . . . . . . . . . . . . . . . . . .

. . . . . . . . . . . . . . . . . . . . . . . . . . . . . . . . . . . . . . . . . . . . .

. . . . . . . . . . . . . . . . . . . . . . . . . . . . . . . . . . . . . . . . . . . . .

. . . . . . . . . . . . . . . . . . . . . . . . . . . . . . . . . . . . . . . . . . . . .

. . . . . . . . . . . . . . . . . . . . . . . . . . . . . . . . . . . . . . . . . . . . .

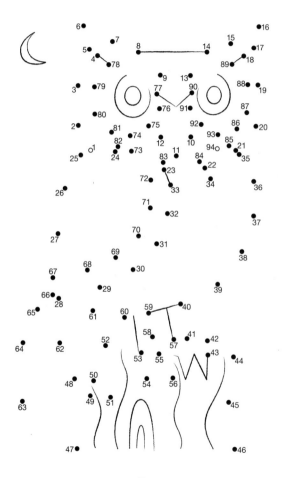

# journal prompt

It can be helpful to your mindfulness practice to write down your thoughts as you have them. Spend a minute or two doing a mindfulness exercise and jot down whatever comes to your mind while you do so.

. . . . . . . . . . . . . . . . . . . . . . . . . . . . . . . . . . . . . . . . . . . . .

. . . . . . . . . . . . . . . . . . . . . . . . . . . . . . . . . . . . . . . . . . . . .

. . . . . . . . . . . . . . . . . . . . . . . . . . . . . . . . . . . . . . . . . . . . .

. . . . . . . . . . . . . . . . . . . . . . . . . . . . . . . . . . . . . . . . . . . . .

. . . . . . . . . . . . . . . . . . . . . . . . . . . . . . . . . . . . . . . . . . . . .

. . . . . . . . . . . . . . . . . . . . . . . . . . . . . . . . . . . . . . . . . . . . .

. . . . . . . . . . . . . . . . . . . . . . . . . . . . . . . . . . . . . . . . . . . . .

. . . . . . . . . . . . . . . . . . . . . . . . . . . . . . . . . . . . . . . . . . . . .

"To be happy—one must find one's bliss."

—*Gloria Vanderbilt*

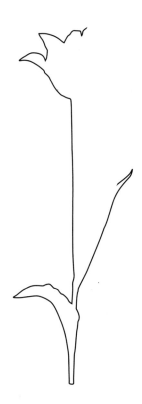

# Friends By Will Nediger

## ACROSS

1. Animal that becomes a chef in a 2007 Pixar film
4. Long-legged wading bird
8. "The Simpsons" storekeeper
9. Got up
11. Feeling between friends
14. Self-evident truth
15. Finished
17. Military school newbie
20. University URL finisher
21. Feeling between friends
24. Women's World Cup powerhouse
25. Closes tight
26. "Private Dancer" singer Turner
28. Nailing, as a test
31. Feeling between friends
34. Modify
35. Hush-hush org.
36. Change the decor of
37. Hardly a social butterfly

## DOWN

1. Nickname for tennis star Nadal
2. High point
3. Dutch flower craze of the 17th century
4. Chemical cousins
5. "Incidentally," in a text
6. Apple's phones run on it
7. Gentrified NYC district
10. Pastimes
12. 1970 hit by the Kinks
13. Mani-___
16. Regret
18. Exclamation from Scrooge
19. Facebook cofounder Saverin
21. Movie director's cry
22. Yard sale stipulation
23. Engrave
27. Relaxing YouTube video genre
29. Snack
30. Greeting Down Under
32. Golf course peg
33. Appropriate answer to the last clue in this crossword

"Live with intention.
Walk to the edge.
Listen hard. Practice
wellness. Play with
abandon."

—*Mary Anne Radmacher*

```
W Y R C A A K S C L O H S T L N D U S A
O X K Z U S G P F H D N O K I U O C I K
H A Q I H B H B M F Y Q B D T K W P A E
W V F X T A Z O R B I Q C Q L Q N M X T
W P E A C B T V U E S E D R E U W O M T
K B M R A R M H P L A A R X U I A U H Q
T J T R P I O J A Y D T P C T Z R N Z C
X P B L L D L W S U J E H D E K D T W G
U O P S A G D E H B P I R E Y E D A A B
C P X E N E H I C O D B V S L A O I R M
W E Q A K C G A R L A N D B T P G N R N
R A Q T T N J F Z S K W A P P A Q H I F
S I D E A N G L E F K T L S O X N J O B
Z G R D F L E X I B I L I T Y S S D R X
Q T R T N H M P C T S S L O L Q E W P Q
S T L W P F B H I G H L U N G E Y S I J
R R J I Z P H T R I A N G L E Y O K G G
A E I S O P U C Y V J B P K X T V J E P
E E D T Z F M M F D M H X C M A E V O Y
D J M M K Z L D Y F G H C H I L D S N Y
```

yoga

BREATHE
BRIDGE
CAT
CHILD'S
COBRA
CROW
DOWNWARD DOG
FIERCE
FLEXIBILITY

GARLAND
HATHA
HIGH LUNGE
MAT
MOUNTAIN
PIGEON
PLANK
POSES
SEATED TWIST

SHOULDER STAND
SIDE ANGLE
STRETCHES
TABLE
TREE
TRIANGLE
WARRIOR

```
H  N  O  S  E  K  Y  J  F  O  O  T
X  A  B  A  C  C  O  R  D  B  Z  J
H  Z  N  O  K  V  J  P  E  E  P  K
E  J  K  D  N  C  Y  A  I  A  O  V
A  A  W  A  K  E  W  R  L  G  O  C
D  A  T  H  E  N  S  I  L  L  D  H
S  E  T  T  E  R  X  S  O  E  L  I
F  A  C  E  K  N  E  E  C  V  E  N
```

## find and circle

| | |
|---|---|
| Eight four-letter parts of the body | ⊘○○○○○○○ |
| Four six-letter dogs | ○○○○ |
| Two European capitals | ○○ |
| Six-letter Honda model | ○ |
| Not asleep | ○ |

42

"Today is only one day in all the days that will ever be. But what will happen in all the other days that ever come can depend on what you do today."

—*Ernest Hemingway*

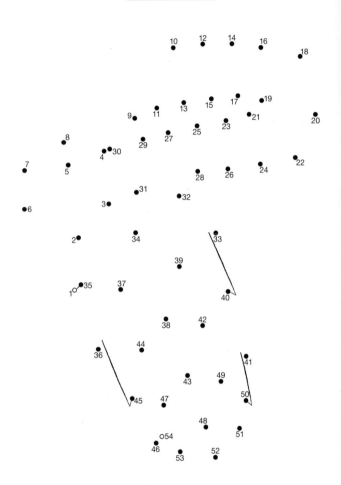

45

"Almost everything will work again if you unplug it for a few minutes, including you."

—*Anne Lamott*

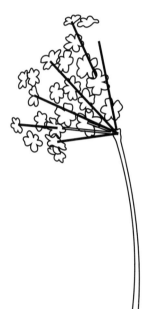

# GIVING BACK By Will Nediger

## ACROSS

1. White on "Wheel of Fortune"
6. Lamb and ham
11. "That is to say ..."
12. Sailing on the briny
13. Local volunteering spot
15. Screw up
16. "Y.M.C.A." and "The Star-Spangled Banner," e.g.
17. Blacken on the grill
19. Thousand bucks
20. Local volunteering spot
23. Plant with pods
24. Piglets' moms
27. Informer
31. "Am I glad to see ___!"
32. Local volunteering spot
34. Diminish
35. Exploited, as the system
36. Powerful winds
37. 1953 western with the plea "Come back!"

## DOWN

1. Workbench grippers
2. When the moon hits your eye like a big pizza pie, e.g.
3. ___ net (deep learning tool)
4. Quick recharge
5. Paul who wrote the lyrics to "My Way"
6. Country star Kathy
7. Some printmakers
8. Tennis legend Arthur
9. Abound
10. Comic ___
14. Deeply embed
18. Witty comeback
21. Contradicts
22. Cellist with a Presidential Medal of Freedom
25. Believe ___ (#MeToo slogan)
26. Luxurious leather
27. Minor setback
28. Marching band behemoth
29. Like some exams
30. Omelet needs
33. "As if!"

"Love yourself first,
and everything else
falls in line. You really
have to love yourself
to get anything done
in this world."

—*Lucille Ball*

```
K K Q A R Q A V B S U M M E R Q O N A T
I V S A S W W X F S H O R E K T E L Q O
C E U T C B K G S Y T M C K F E L I D W
K X N G O I A O S O S G P R R E P F N E
B H G W O K E O H C T U U C R U O K J L
A A L N L I M D E P V S S B P Y B Y J Z
C T A X E N R B L L D N M F K I E A J B
K B S Z R I O O L E U U I L C N Y V X B
S B S E P B Z O S S H A H I N B D Y C O
W O E V Q Y A K X C V Y V P P V X J A O
I D S L I S I R A F G M P F Z E G P S G
M Y W Q I J X E E N R V O L Q I W S A I
A B Y A V F B P O F R K B O Z U S Q N E
E O R Z I O E R C K O Z X P S H W H D B
G A L V S E A G P X K O I S N L N G C O
L R C L O S J E U B A D T N A Q C P A A
I D M M R F E R Q A J Y M Z C O T R S R
H W C O V E R U P P R U U W K S T F T D
L H K N S H O R T S V D Y K S H N D L W
R D P S U N S H I N E O I H T W A V E S
```

## beach day

BAREFOOT
BEACH UMBRELLA
BIKINI
BODY BOARD
BOOGIE BOARD
COVER-UP
COOLER
FLIP-FLOPS
GOOD BOOK
HAT

KICK BACK
LIFEGUARD
SANDCASTLE
SARONG
SHELLS
SHORE
SHORTS
SNACKS
SUMMER
SUNGLASSES

SUNSCREEN
SUNSHINE
SURF
SWIM
TOWEL
VISOR
WAVES
ZINC

# mindful listening

We acclimate to the sounds around us and often tune them out. Try some mindful listening. If you are outside, try to tune in to the sounds you hear. It could be the wind through the trees, birds chirping, even sirens—whatever is happening around you in the present moment. To add more intention to this exercise, put on some music and really *listen*. Try not to think about things such as lyrics, but instead experience the sounds as they happen.

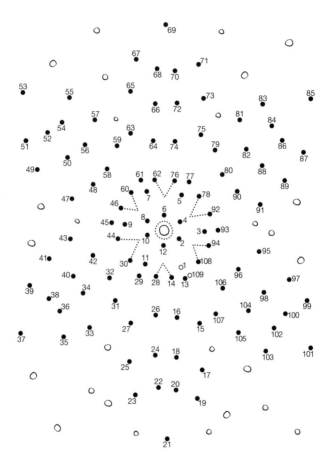

```
W C R O B I N J A P A N
Z R E E G Y P T Y N F G
S O E A P E C K R I A O
Y W J N G Y K O A U L L
L Y A B Z L D V I G C D
A X K N B N E E D N O U
T S M O O C H R N E N C
I K J C H I N A I P Z K
```

## find and circle

| | |
|---|---|
| Nine birds | ⊘○○○○○○○○ |
| Five five-letter countries | ○○○○○ |
| Two words that mean "kiss" | ○○ |
| Opposite of under | ○ |
| Medal for a first-place finisher | ○ |

57

"Nourishing yourself in a
way that helps you blossom
in the direction you want to
go is attainable, and you are
worth the effort."

—*Deborah Day*

# MEDITATION By Will Nediger

## ACROSS

1. Honoree on the second Sunday in May
4. Loud-buzzing insects
11. Pie ___ mode
12. Someone who believes the world is made up of tiny particles
13. "That's amazing!", in a text
14. Tallinn's country
15. Parts of a Clue board
17. Practical joke
18. Line on a weather map
20. Tag along
21. Pleasant emanation from a coffee shop
23. "I'll have what ___ having"
26. Weapon-shaped desserts
30. Cute toy dog breed, for short
31. Transform
32. Perfect example
36. Patriotic chant at the Olympics
37. Fill with a crayon
38. Bit of Oscar recognition, informally
39. Openly show contempt for
40. Meditation syllables (one of which is found in every row of this crossword)

## DOWN

1. New Zealand native
2. Actor Edward James ___
3. Myopic Mr. in cartoons
4. Salad with croutons
5. "___ a Wonderful Life"
6. Simple bed
7. "Te ___" (Spanish "I love you")
8. Dog from Down Under
9. Hit 2007 Alicia Keys album
10. Place for a play
16. Degrees for CEOs
19. Steal from
20. Green/earth-toned pattern, for short
22. Heartbeat
23. Design deets
24. Motorcyclist's invitation
25. Zola or Hirsch
27. Mars of "Uptown Funk"
28. ___ salts (ingredient in a relaxing bath)
29. Pillow covers
33. Wiggler on a foot
34. Hockey legend Bobby
35. "Mamma ___!"

"Self-care is how you take
your power back."

—*Lalah Delia*

```
T  K  T  U  R  K  E  Y  K  L  P  S
Z  R  Z  A  R  V  S  R  W  O  I  O
G  J  E  O  T  I  J  A  T  N  T  D
R  U  P  E  R  H  S  V  E  D  A  A
O  I  Z  A  K  R  E  E  R  O  L  P
V  C  P  L  A  C  E  N  N  N  I  E
E  E  K  W  R  E  N  J  S  Z  A  E
M  A  D  R  I  D  S  W  A  N  N  L
```

## find and circle

| | |
|---|---|
| Orange _____ | ⊘○○○○ |
| Five European capitals | ○○○○○ |
| Four birds ending in "N" | ○○○○ |
| _____ sausage | ○○○ |
| Monopoly space: Park _____ | ○ |

"When you undervalue
what you do, the world will
undervalue who you are."

—*Oprah Winfrey*

```
X P Q S L R I N A G O I A I I X U P X N
D K M T B H X Y T E X S O V P O W L W O
I O E K H E E P H B S E Y O B P B A P E
K F T C I R O I E R U O L U D O L U P D
T Z A L P A R L O R V T P E H Y X T C I
I I M O P C Y I G I W Q G S M W S U Z P
A M O U O L Z A O Q Q R E I F E L S Z U
L E R D C E Y D N V Q M E F T A N Y E S
C D P S R S I Z Y Y A I L E H J B T O Y
E E H J A V J R S G F U L O I X C L S F
S A O U T N W W L D W B M Y S X K Y E Z
T G S J I V T I E O I A K V T Q C S U S
I V I B C P G I E B R Z P S O W X K R P
S N S A C F E B G T T O P C R G Q G N D
W O C C O K M N C O H E R O I D E S I P
Z T A C R B M E G T N J S Z E D Y W P L
T K I H P Z L M Y Q V E N N S T E P F V
E P W U U E S G I L G A M E S H I R H E
E O W S S M M W Z I G O I D V H Z C Z M
S Y M P O S I U M R E P U B L I C T S N
```

## classical literature

AESOP'S FABLES
ALCESTIS
ANTIGONE
BACCHUS
BEOWULF
BIBLE
CLOUDS
ELECTRA
ELEMENTS

EPIC OF
   GILGAMESH
GILGAMESH
HERACLES
HEROIDES
HIPPOCRATIC
   CORPUS
HISTORIES
ILIAD
MEDEA

METAMORPHOSIS
ODYSSEY
OEDIPUS
PLAUTUS
POETICS
REPUBLIC
SYMPOSIUM
THEOGONY

```
T Z E L E C T R O N P Z
H U Z E R O R N C O R I
J L B Z B A I O N J O N
B I V A T L J A J L T C
U M K I O N I Z C E O D
G E U I A P A I R M N R
L G V B N E U T R O N U
E T R O M B O N E N Z M
```

## find and circle

| | |
|---|---|
| Eight musical instruments | ⊘○○○○○○○ |
| Three parts of an atom | ○○○ |
| Two citrus fruits | ○○ |
| Two four-letter words starting with "Z" | ○○ |
| Two of a kind | ○ |

68

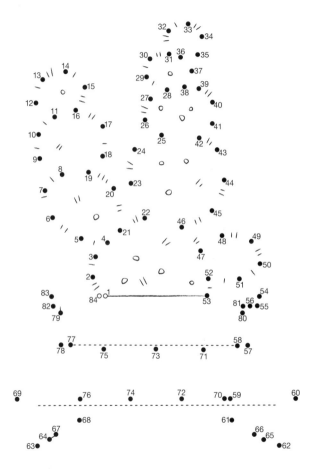

# get outside

Try to engage all of your senses next time you step outside. Notice the contours and textures of the things you see. Allow the sounds you hear to wash over you. Tune in to the sensation of fresh air on your skin. Spending mindful time in nature—even if it's just a walk around the block—will improve attention, reduce anxiety, and boost happiness.

"Everyone shines,
given the right
lighting."

—*Susan Cain*

```
F Y P A T I E N T S X S
L I G R E E N Z S S R B
L F V J K S Y R E E Z R
U U Z E S T O S K E K O
P L X E N T R C G C L W
O L H E C U E I A L J N
N C W O N H E L U K E C
E T D Z C B B D Z T X B
```

## find and circle

| | |
|---|---|
| Common denominations of U.S. currency | ⊘ ○ ○ ○ |
| Four five-letter colors | ○ ○ ○ ○ |
| Three groups of people in a hospital | ○ ○ ○ |
| Three four-letter words ending in "ULL" | ○ ○ ○ |
| Two games played on the same board | ○ ○ |

74

"If it doesn't challenge
you, it won't change you."

—*Fred DeVito*

# SELF-HELP By Will Nediger

## ACROSS

1. "1, 2 Step" singer
6. Defeat handily
11. Capital of Jordan
12. "Family Matters" nerd
13. Author of the self-help book "The Power"
15. Many a concert souvenir
16. Staple crop in Nigeria
17. Put two and two together?
18. Spheres in the sky
20. Cool
22. Norman Vincent who wrote the self-help book "The Power of Positive Thinking"
24. Eckhart who wrote the self-help book "The Power of Now"
28. Initials in French fashion
30. Opportunity, metaphorically
31. Ostrich relative
34. Hawaiian or Samoan dish
36. India's smallest state
37. Author of the self-help book "Unlimited Power"
40. "Me too," way more formally
41. Bert's roommate
42. "Huzzah!", e.g.
43. Stun gun

## DOWN

1. Like carriers that go on the roof
2. Announcement upon arriving
3. Organism under a microscope
4. Hightailed it
5. Warhol who was shot by Valerie Solanas
6. Button on the last page of an online application
7. Give it a go
8. Gumbo veggie
9. Patch or darn
10. Begged
14. Sound at a spa
19. Cunning
21. Pea jacket?
23. ___ de corps
25. Computer sign-ons
26. Canadian coin nicknamed for a bird
27. Whiteboard cleaner
29. British facilities
31. Airport guesses, for short
32. Dance in a pit
33. Ctrl+Z
35. "A likely story!"
38. The solver of this crossword
39. Nursing product

78

"Remember always
that you not only
have the right to be
an individual, you
have an obligation
to be one."

—*Eleanor Roosevelt*

M S T O O D Y B L O O D
B I Z X C K T X Y J N J
K T L J J H R R F Z E L
M O J K G E E O O Z W O
A A Z O T V O E X O T O
E D R T B L U E S H P R
R F U M A B R U C E J D
C B V K G Y O G U R T Z

## find and circle

| | |
|---|---|
| Five dairy products | ⊘○○○○ |
| Five five-letter words containing "OO" | ○○○○○ |
| Three amphibians | ○○○ |
| Willis or Lee | ○ |
| Five-letter style of music | ○ |

# 7-11 breathing

It's not just the name of a convenience store chain.
7-11 breathing promotes relaxation and composure
and it couldn't be simpler. Just breathe in for a count
of seven and out for a count of eleven. Inhale for
seven; exhale for eleven. Keep it going until you're
calm in mind and body. You've got this!

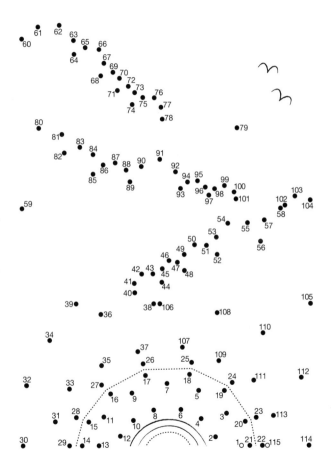

"We all have different
gifts, so we all have
different ways of saying
to the world who we are."

—*Fred Rogers*

# single-pointed concentration

With its roots in Buddhist meditation, single-pointed concentration is a meditation practice that is helpful for clearing your mind. Choose your focus point or object—it can be something meaningful, such as a memento from a loved one, or whatever you have at hand, such as a pen or a specific spot on the wall in front of you. Try to focus all your attention on your point, clearing your mind of distraction. If your mind begins to wander, simply bring your attention back to your object. Single-pointed concentration is a great way to practice finding peace in the moment.

# WRITING By Will Nediger

## ACROSS

1. Some cameras, for short
5. Sparkly stone
10. Studied at school
11. ___ orange
12. After the bell
13. "What's ___?" (response to a classic prank)
14. Adam and 28 Down's home
15. Meddle
16. Bowling variety with a small ball
18. Nowhere to be found, for short
21. Aptly-named author who emphasized the importance of writing in "The Self Care Revolution"
23. Angsty genre
24. Disney World home
25. You might slide into them online
26. Nuisance
27. Outfit
30. Waterfall mist
31. Something to RSVP to on Facebook
32. Gung-ho
33. Tires spring them
34. Partner of "crafts" or "humanities"

## DOWN

1. Rock concert venue
2. Medici family member nicknamed "the Magnificent"
3. King or Dangerfield
4. Sun spot?
5. Place to write a gratitude list, for example
6. Catch a glimpse of
7. Chunk of cash
8. Swelled head
9. Part of an itinerary
12. In need of a massage
15. Wharves
17. Nudges that help with writer's block
18. Tower on a mosque
19. Delhi residents, e.g.
20. What a long wait might feel like
22. Smartly dressed
25. Drop in milk
27. Hairspray alternative
28. Major character in Genesis
29. Drink in a cozy
30. Jamaican music genre

"It's up to us to choose
contentment and
thankfulness."

—*Joanna Gaines*

```
S  H  J  K  S  G  E  O  R  G  E  S
J  H  Y  O  Y  L  E  Z  K  X  V  N
W  L  O  J  H  G  I  L  Y  D  O  E
E  U  X  E  N  N  A  P  N  Z  G  A
H  A  B  A  V  D  K  O  P  K  N  K
S  P  R  B  N  Y  M  K  X  E  I  E
A  O  C  A  K  L  H  I  G  H  R  R
C  Z  S  V  A  P  U  R  P  L  E  Z
```

## find and circle

| | |
|---|---|
| Four things worn on the foot starting with "S" | ⨀○○○ |
| The Beatles (first names) | ○○○○ |
| Two six-letter colors | ○○ |
| Two six-letter nuts | ○○ |
| Opposite of low | ○ |

93

"If you don't go after what you want, you'll never have it. If you don't ask, the answer is always no. If you don't step forward, you're always in the same place."

—Nora Roberts

```
B C P Y S F L E X I B I L I T Y E A S D
I T R L J K I C K B O X I N G L S K N F
C P C O P R P I L A T E S R C Y Y V N V
Y H A L S I S I X Q S W E Y C R K O M L
C T R P J S Q T Q D W P C K T P I Q X J
L B D P F X C R R R I I E H P T A L D G
E A I C N W E O Q E B N T E A G O Y W T
A L O T G W E W U Y T G T N D Z C W U E
J A V O O R N I R N N C I E Y N Y J M N
T N A P U G O A G E T D H K R O E Q U N
R C S B H F N W R H R R W I W V G D W I
K E C O W O Q T I O T S Y W N T A A J S
M W U P I K S N O N T T W S F G N L D C
B E L T J Z K C T O G U R I K K K M S O
S N A V D A C C U R A C Y A M I M Y M U
B T R E L C R V N K A R N B I M I P J R
S N W A G I L I T Y J C K W E N I N F T
R U N N I N G P J J A E K Z E Q I N G V
Y O J D P P M N S T A M I N A U W N G D
Q C I R C U I T T R A I N I N G U X G I
```

## exercise

ACCURACY
AGILITY
BALANCE
BICYCLE
CARDIOVASCULAR
CIRCUIT TRAINING
COORDINATION
CROSS-COUNTRY
   SKIING

FLEXIBILITY
INTERVALS
KICKBOXING
PILATES
POWER
ROWING
RUNNING
SPEED
STAMINA

STATIONARY
   BICYCLE
STRENGTH
STRETCHING
SWIMMING
TENNIS COURT
TRACK
WEIGHT TRAINING
YOGA

"I will breathe. I will think of
solutions. I will not let my worry
control me. I will not let my
stress level break me. I will
simply breathe."

—*Shayne McClendon*

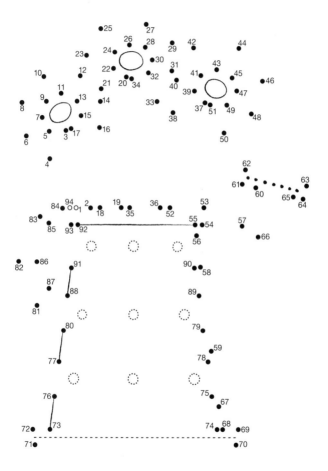

# mindful self-love

So much of mindfulness practice revolves around refocusing on the present moment while our minds try to wander. It's important to forgive ourselves for these distractions. Mindfulness is all about short-circuiting unhelpful thought patterns, and negative self-talk is a big one. None of us are perfect. It's so important not only to accept the present moment for what it is, but accept ourselves for who we are. Acknowledge any distractions, forgive yourself for them, and bring your focus back.

"Choose, everyday, to forgive yourself. You are human, flawed, and most of all worthy of love."

—*Alison Malee*

# YOGA By Will Nediger

**ACROSS**

1. Fruit-filled pastry
8. Go downhill fast?
11. Australia's region
12. Huge amount
13. Yoga pose with a militaristic name
14. Gave the green light
15. Fibs
16. Barbershop quartet member
18. Neighborhood in a classic bossa nova song
20. Yoga pose with a canine name
24. Binge-watching segment
25. Like a tofu burger with non-dairy cheese
26. Bruins' school
30. Verb suffix
31. Yoga pose with a cetacean name
34. Word before Peep, Kim, or Nas X, in music
35. Exam in which you might have to squint
36. Messy room
37. Comebacks

**DOWN**

1. Prominent bloodhound feature
2. Berry often promoted for its antioxidants
3. Simple
4. Old salts
5. DiFranco of folk
6. Brazilian city home to 18-Across
7. Steak ___ (raw dish)
8. "Everybody must get ___" (Bob Dylan lyric)
9. Relaxing place in a Beach Boys song
10. Like performers on a RuPaul reality show
17. Conclusion
18. "Hmm ..."
19. Bachelor's home
20. Imps
21. Gift-giver's excite exclamation
22. Squirming around
23. Code-cracking org.
26. As many as
27. One-named singer with a delightful Twitter presence
28. Aid for Santa
29. Tiny hill builders
32. Spanish "Listen up!"
33. Give permission to

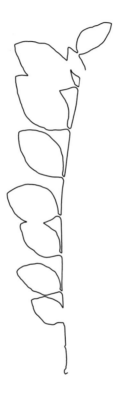

"Life offers you a thousand chances . . . all you have to do is take one."

—*Frances Mayes*

# notes

........................................................

........................................................

........................................................

........................................................

........................................................

........................................................

........................................................

........................................................

........................................................

........................................................

........................................................

........................................................

# notes

solutions

# SOLUTIONS

3   word search

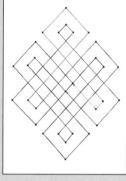

5   dot to dot

10   spot the differences

| H | A | Y | E | K |   | M | O | D | A | L |
|---|---|---|---|---|---|---|---|---|---|---|
| A | S | O | N | E |   | O | H | A | R | A |
| N | O | U | R | I | S | H | M | E | N | T |
|   | F | R | I | T | O | S |   | W | O | K |
|   |   | Q | E | D |   | M | O | L | E |   |
|   | S | O | U | L |   | F | O | O | D |   |
| H | O | L | E |   | P | A | N |   |   |   |
| E | N | D |   | A | R | R | I | B | A |   |
| H | O | M | E | C | O | O | K | I | N | G |
| I | M | A | G | E |   | F | E | D | T | O |
| M | A | N | O | R |   | F | R | E | E | D |

12   crossword

114

15 word search

FLORENCE, PALERMO,

VENICE, NAPLES,

GENOA, MILAN,

ROME—INDIGO, PURPLE,

YELLOW, ORANGE,

VIOLET—MAYOR—

ALOHA—PLANT

16 word roundup

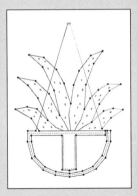

19 dot to dot

24 spot the differences

26  crossword

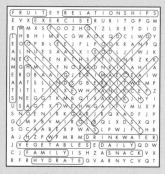

29  word search

31  dot to dot

36  spot the differences

38 crossword

41 word search

HAND, HEAD, FACE,

KNEE, CHIN, FOOT,

NOSE, BONE—

POODLE, BEAGLE,

COLLIE, SETTER—

ATHENS, PARIS—

ACCORD—AWAKE

42 word roundup

44 dot to dot

48  spot the differences

50  crossword

53  word search

55  dot to dot

PENGUIN, FALCON,
CONDOR, EAGLE,
ROBIN, DUCK, SWAN,
CROW, WREN—INDIA,
CHINA, EGYPT, ITALY,
JAPAN—SMOOCH,
PECK—OVER—GOLD

57  word roundup

60  spot the differences

| M | O | M |   | C | I | C | A | D | A | S |
|---|---|---|---|---|---|---|---|---|---|---|
| A | L | A |   | A | T | O | M | I | S | T |
| O | M | G |   | E | S | T | O | N | I | A |
| R | O | O | M | S |   |   | G | A | G |   |
| I | S | O | B | A | R |   | C | O | M | E |
|   |   | A | R | O | M | A |   |   |   |   |
| S | H | E | S |   | B | O | M | B | E | S |
| P | O | M |   |   | M | O | R | P | H |   |
| E | P | I | T | O | M | E |   | U | S | A |
| C | O | L | O | R | I | N |   | N | O | M |
| S | N | E | E | R | A | T |   | O | M | S |

62  crossword

GROVE, JUICE, SODA,
PEEL, TREE—LONDON,
ATHENS, MADRID,
WARSAW, PARIS—
RAVEN, SWAN, WREN,
TERN—ITALIAN,
TURKEY, PORK—PLACE

65  word roundup

67 word search

TROMBONE, GUITAR,
VIOLIN, BUGLE, BANJO,
PIANO, TUBA, DRUM—
ELECTRON, NEUTRON,
PROTON—LEMON,
LIME—ZINC, ZERO—
PAIR

68 word roundup

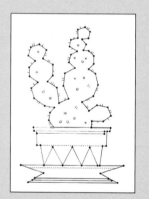

69 dot to dot

TWENTY, FIVE, TEN,
ONE—GREEN, BEIGE,
BROWN, BLACK—
PATIENTS, DOCTORS,
NURSES—PULL, FULL,
DULL—CHECKERS,
CHESS

74 word roundup

# SOLUTIONS

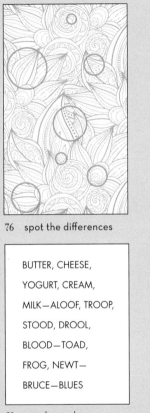

76  spot the differences

| C | I | A | R | A |   |   | S | T | O | M | P |
|---|---|---|---|---|---|---|---|---|---|---|---|
| A | M | M | A | N |   |   | U | R | K | E | L |
| R | H | O | N | D | A | B | Y | R | N | E |   |
| T | E | E |   | Y | A | M |   | A | D | D |   |
| O | R | B | S |   | H | I | P |   |   |   |   |
| P | E | A | L | E |   | T | O | L | L | E |   |
|   |   | Y | S | L |   | D | O | O | R |   |   |
| E | M | U |   | P | O | I |   | G | O | A |   |
| T | O | N | Y | R | O | B | B | I | N | S |   |
| A | S | D | O | I |   | E | R | N | I | E |   |
| S | H | O | U | T |   | T | A | S | E | R |   |

78  crossword

BUTTER, CHEESE,
YOGURT, CREAM,
MILK—ALOOF, TROOP,
STOOD, DROOL,
BLOOD—TOAD,
FROG, NEWT—
BRUCE—BLUES

81  word roundup

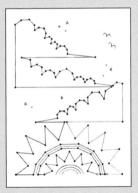

83  dot to dot

88  spot the differences

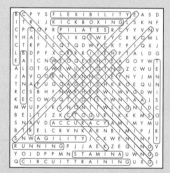

90  crossword

SNEAKER,

SLIPPER, SANDAL,

SHOE—GEORGE,

RINGO, JOHN,

PAUL—ORANGE,

PURPLE—CASHEW,

ALMOND—HIGH

93  word roundup

95  word search

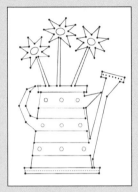

97 dot to dot

102 spot the differences

104 crossword

108 spot the differences